Robots Plan Vacations

How I Used Artificial Intelligence to Plan My Travels

Angelina Allsop

Traveling Monsters Publishing House

Download the Free Companion Guide

Y ou can put your notepad and pen away. There's no need to take notes, cause I've put all the prompts and resources together into a convenient swipesheet.

Download the free companion guide at RobotsDoStuff.com

Thanks for reading!!

Book Title: Robots Plan My Vacations: How I Use Artificial Intelligence to Plan My Travels

Series: Robots Do Stuff

Written by: Angelina Allsop

Published by Traveling Monsters Publishing House

Traveling Monsters Publishing House

TravelingMonsters.com

Free Books, Audiobooks, Printables, and more @ AngelinaAllsop.com

Cover by: Angelina Allsop

Cover Elements by: Vecteezy & Envato Elements

Printed in the USA & UK

1st Edition

To my funny, sexy, wonderful hubby who lets me drag him all over the world.

Contents

Chapter One

AI Played in My Sandbox

N ot gonna lie... I thought I would have some time before AI stole my job...

I was wrong.

It was April 2023 when I learned I wouldn't have any income. The client I worked for, a marketing agency that had been more or less my sole source of income for the better part of two years, announced ChatGPT had taken over 40% of their clients in the last four months.

What had been once the stuff of science fiction was here and on the computers of every student, entrepreneur, marketer, and more. ChatGPT had been released the November, before and it was already gunning for my job - mine - the one I thought would always need a human to do. I naively thought AI wouldn't play in my sandbox. Humans would do human things, like art, and robots can do boring robot things like... I dunno... data entry. But, here it was, trying to take—nope, TAKING my job.

Naturally, I did what any person would do. I panicked.

I cried.

I complained.

I threw a fit.

I was scared, sick to my stomach... and yet, no matter how long I cried, AI would not go away.

Ok, time for Plan B: Infiltrate.

There are times in history when innovation comes and forces people to pay attention. As queasy as this invention made me, I knew in my bones it was here to stay. I needed to learn this new tool or find a new career.

A little backstory, until 2021, I had gone from soulless job to soulless job. I had FINALLY built enough courage to go for my dream of writing full time, and a mere two years later, I was watching it get taken away.

Nope. Time to adapt. I had worked too hard for too long to let my dream career slip away. I couldn't bury my head in the sand. AI was not to be ignored.

I started experimenting with AI and... I'm not gonna lie. I was FRUSTRATED. It was annoying, especially as a writing tool. But one day, everything changed.

I was texting a friend heading to Barcelona, and she was asking me to help her find where to stay.

My husband and I have always been big travelers. After the pandemic, we made the switch to full-time travel. Because of my love and experience with traveling, I became my friends' unofficial travel agent. Anytime anyone had a travel-related question, they came to me. So, naturally, when my friend wanted to check out a new spot, she asked me for recommendations.

The difference now was I was busier than I had been in a while. I didn't have the same time to plan everyone else's- and even my own travels. I had ChatGPT open, so I let it do some of the heavy lifting.

I was floored by the results...

Chapter Two

How to Use This Book

Who is this book for?

First off, this book is NOT for those looking to build an AI-based travel business.

You don't have to be a coder, tech-savvy person, or expert traveler.

This book is for the average person who wants their own travel agent they can put in their pocket and pull out whenever they want to plan a vacation or have a travel-related question.

It's for the busy moms...
The entrepreneurs with a packed calendar...
The family man trying to create memories...
The one stuck planning the yearly family reunion with a million spinning plates

to consider...

If you're an average Joe or Josephine trying to travel better, without spending a ton of time planning or breaking the bank, **this book is for you.**

This isn't a tech-heavy guide.

My goal is for you to learn how to travel better & longer using AI to do so, but I won't be giving you too many step-by-step instructions on the technicalities of ChatGPT. There are too many updates going on right now. It's likely I would tell you to "go to the top, left-hand corner and select settings" and by the time the book comes out, the settings are in the bottom, right-hand corner. Inaccurate instructions like that frustrate me, and I don't want to do the same to you.

What I will do is dive deep into the process behind using AI so you can successfully plan your trip under any ChatGPT version update.

Take what you need. Ditch the rest.

I designed this book to be no longer than exactly the information you need. I made it short on purpose. I carefully thought through every word, cutting any fluff, but there are still going to be things you might feel are irrelevant. If so, skip it. You won't hurt my feelings.

RobotsDoStuff.com

I invite you to steal my ChatGPT prompts, travel resources, and favorite gear list. This resource will save you a ton of time. Good prompts can sometimes be long and tedious to write and most people will charge you to use theirs. You can get a copy of the prompts I use in this book, and more, sent to your email for free by going to RobotsDoStuff.com

Chapter Three

The Vietnam Balcony... and Other Meltdowns

What is AI?

I had a few minutes before I needed to leave the house. Ok, cool. Let's give ChatGPT a simple task. Something that will save me a ton of time but shouldn't be too complex.

For those of you who don't know me, I am an author of fiction books in addition to this non-fiction book series. I had written a (rather excellent) book for 8-10 year-olds called *How to Tell if Your Grandma is a Vampire*. I had taken a bit of a risk and wrote it in 1st person. After I wrote the entire book and I was working on the second book, I was second guessing if this was a wise move. ...but I had a handy virtual assistant in my pocket, right? Right???

It was supposed to be a super simple task. "GPT, bud, convert this chapter from 1st person to 3rd person. Come on, man." Nothing I did — and I mean nothing, could get it to do what I asked it to do. It kept changing a large percentage of the text "improving it" for me, when in reality, it was making it more appealing for an adult reading sales material. FYI, kids are so NOT into that.

I finally came inside from sitting on the patio for an hour trying to figure it out. I was in tears and venting to my hubby, who listened, a bemused look on his face. He teased me for being stinky (I had been outside in Vietnam's summer heat yelling at my computer), kissed my nose, and told me I would figure it out and not to get frustrated.

Consider this chapter, my kiss on your nose. ChatGPT will probably act the fool. Try not to get frustrated. Think of it like hiring a bored high schooler to do your busy work for you. It'll probably figure out 80-90% of what you need — more if you learn *how* it works.

ChatGPT can be like a free (or pretty cheap) virtual assistant if you let it. The catch is that it comes with almost no human intuition.

None.

Nada.

So, when there's a problem or a question, where a human can guess and typically "figure it out", ChatGPT *kinda* can't. It's programmed to do what it's told to do and think what it's ordered to think about.

But... taking the time to teach it how to think and how best to respond to you could save you a TON of time. Fortunately for you, I put my sweat and tears into this project (literally, because of my crying session on my Vietnam patio). I did all the trial and error for you.

Your Expert(ish) Guide

I want to note that I am not an expert. Frankly, anyone, except those who invented AI, who poses themselves as an expert, is KINDA lying. AI is SOOOO new, and it's changing every day.

I have, however, taken the time to learn HOW to use AI to save time planning my travels. Because I am a full-time digital nomad, planning my travels can take a significant amount of time. There are so many little nuances that can throw wrenches in plans — just ask any traveler about visas and they'll give you an earful.

I am not a perfect travel expert, but I have helped a lot of my friends save a TON of time and money on their trips and now, I'd like to do the same for you.

So, what is AI, anyway?

First off, ChatGPT is not a sentient being. Not sure if that disappoints you or not, but the AI powering ChatGPT is called Natural Language Processing (NLP), which is a process that merely pretends at human intelligence.

Though I picture it as an alien, it's closer to a parrot who mimics human speech, and honestly, a parrot is closer to sentient than ChatGPT.

It can "learn", but it's only learning what words to mimic back to make you happy. It cannot truly understand what it's telling you — not yet, at least. One day soon, probably, but for now, you need to learn how to tell it what words to tell you. Make sense? If not, don't worry, it will as you move along with this book.

Priming & Prompts

Priming your AI and writing effective prompts will be the two most impactful skills you can deploy to get better results from your AI. I will go into more detail in the future, but essentially, this is how you tell ChatGPT what you want. There's a surprising amount that goes into this.

It might go rogue...

Like I said, earlier, it's important to know ChatGPT is probably gonna make a couple of mistakes. Sometimes those mistakes are wild and seemingly out of nowhere.

But, think about it...

It's sourcing nearly all of its information from blogs. The trouble is, you can literally write whatever you want on a blog. There's not a fact-checking police force out there making sure Google is correct in its search results. However, most of the time, bloggers *will* fact-check because, otherwise, they lose their followers.

But, bloggers and Wiki authors occasionally make mistakes - or their information out there is outdated. Well, this is what ChatGPT is sourcing its information from.... In fact, at the time of writing this book, ChatGPT is sourcing information from September 2021. You can sorta get around referencing old info by upgrading to ChatGPT 4 and using plugins that perform live web searches.

Therefore, if you're using ChatGPT for the entire travel planning process, I highly recommend quickly fact-checking at each stage. Don't worry, it's not as cumbersome as it sounds. I'll give you an example.

I was tired of being hot, (...living in Asia can do that to you) and I wanted to find a cooler place to stay next summer that remained within our limited budget. I asked ChatGPT to generate a list of cities in Non-Schengen Europe or Africa, within my budget, near a beach, and under a certain temperature.

For those of you who do not know this, the Schengen region of Europe (which hosts countries such as Italy, France, Germany, and many more) will only allow travelers to visit for 90 days within a 180-day period. We were planning on traveling to one of the Schengen countries earlier that year, so we needed to be careful of our time there.

I primed ChatGPT and ended with, *"Before we get started, do you have questions for me so you can best understand my needs?"* This question can be the single most impactful trick you do to get ChatGPT to work well for you.

ChatGPT, you are a travel expert specializing in planning vacations for a couple that loves eating in restaurants and walking around a city in NON Schengen Europe or African. Your task is to help me find a city I can summer in with a budget of under 2000. I love walking and taking subways and taking trains through cities and bustling beaches with a lots of restaurants, stunning landscapes, or things to do and trying out local cuisines at mid-range restaurants. I prefer staying in boutique hotels, serviced apartments, and vacation rentals, etc. and using public transportation or walking, etc. to explore the cities or beaches. The cities you suggest should have mild weather, with temperatures ranging between 40 and 83 Fahrenheit during my stay. consider how long a US citizen can stay without needing a visa or with a visa upon arrival. In a minute, I will ask you to suggest a bulleted list that includes the countries I should visit along with recommended cities to stay for a month or more along with the pros and cons of each place. MAKE SURE TO AVOID SCHENGEN ZONE COUNTRIES. Before we get started, do you have any questions for me so you can best understand my needs?

By the way, if you're looking at the prompt and gaping, don't worry, I have swipeable prime and prompts on RobotsDoStuff.com.

 Thank you for providing all the necessary information. I have a clear understanding of your preferences. Before suggesting a list of cities for you to consider, I have a couple of questions:

1. What time of year are you planning to travel? The availability of mild weather can vary depending on the season.
2. Are there any specific cuisines or types of cuisine that you and your partner prefer?
3. Do you have any particular interests or activities you enjoy, such as historical sites, outdoor adventures, or cultural events?

Knowing these details will help me tailor my suggestions to your preferences.

If you'll notice, ChatGPT asked me, "*What time of year are you planning to travel?*" If you're rolling your eyes, you're not alone. In my prompt, I clearly say summer. This is a common problem ChatGPT does right now. My boy is guaranteed to miss a detail or two. That's part of why ending with this question is so important.

Great! Based on your preferences, here is a list of cities outside the Schengen Zone in Europe and Africa that you could consider for your summer vacation. Each city comes with its pros and cons, taking into account your interests, budget, mild weather, and visa requirements:

1. Lisbon, Portugal:
   * Pros: Beautiful architecture, vibrant food scene, mild weather during summer, bustling beaches, and rich historical sites.
   * Cons: Can be crowded during peak tourist season.
2. Split, Croatia:
   * Pros: Stunning coastal city, historic old town, delicious local cuisine, moderate summer temperatures, and easy access to nearby islands.
   * Cons: Can be crowded with tourists, especially in popular areas.
3. Marrakech, Morocco:
   * Pros: Exotic atmosphere, vibrant markets, unique Moroccan cuisine, fascinating historical sites (such as the Medina), warm summer weather, and beautiful landscapes.
   * Cons: High temperatures in summer (can exceed 83°F), potential language barrier.
4. Istanbul, Turkey:
   * Pros: Rich history, magnificent architecture (including the Hagia Sophia and Blue Mosque), diverse culinary scene, pleasant summer weather, and a vibrant atmosphere.
   * Cons: Can be crowded, potential language barrier.
5. Cape Town, South Africa:
   * Pros: Breathtaking landscapes (Table Mountain, Cape Peninsula), diverse cuisine, pleasant summer temperatures, beautiful beaches, and a vibrant cultural scene.
   * Cons: Longer travel distance, potential visa requirements for US citizens (check visa regulations beforehand).
6. Casablanca, Morocco:
   * Pros: Cosmopolitan city, blend of modern and traditional architecture, delicious Moroccan cuisine, mild summer weather, and proximity to beautiful beaches.
   * Cons: Less historical sites compared to other cities on the list.

Remember to check visa requirements for each specific destination as they can vary for US citizens. Additionally, consider the COVID-19 situation and any travel restrictions or entry requirements that may be in place at the time of your trip.

I took a quick glance at the list it generated and immediately noticed a couple of mistakes. Portugal is inside the Schengen Zone, something I didn't want. I also know Croatia is hot in the summer. I selected four from the list that sounded good. At that point, I double-checked the August temperatures and realized one was too hot.

Now, there are a couple of options. I can either go with the three cities that work or have ChatGPT try again. Later in this book, I'll give you some pointers to getting better responses.

Chapter Four
Zip Lining & Other Lies

AI Basics

O k... this might be a SUPER unpopular belief, but I am not a fan of zip lining. Yet, almost every vacation, my friends want to go on one. My brain always tries to convince me it's gonna be fun. Lies. It's never been fun... not one time — for me, at least. But tons of other people LOVE it — my friends included.

So why mention this?

According to Google, bloggers often list zip lining as a "staple" to a "perfect vacation". But if you keep reading through the Google search results, you'll find I am not alone on my mild disdain for zip lining. Keep reading further and you'll learn the "perfect vacation" is different with each blog post you read.

If you look within your friend, family, and coworker groups, you'll probably find someone who believes the only good vacation involves gutting fish, while another won't even entertain a vacation that doesn't involve margaritas and a beach chair.

My point is there are different "types of travel" - RV, tent camping, all-inclusive beach lounging, adventure travel, historical sightseeing, foodie trips, and countless others... What I am trying to get at is, if you ask ChatGPT to "plan a 'great' vacation", the likelihood you get a vacation plan you'd hate is pretty high. If you want ChatGPT to plan the perfect vacation FOR YOU, you gotta be specific...

Priming can help. Let's talk about it.

Chat Threads

Before I get into priming, let's quickly talk about how to set up a ChatGPT account. If you haven't already, hop on over to https://chat.openai.com/ and create an account. You may prefer it on your cellphone. If so, go to your app store and download the ChatGPT app by OpenAI.

When you're logged in, you can hit "New Chat" or "Message" to get started. After you've started to use it, you'll probably notice the chat history shows different chat threads. On the desktop, right now, the historical chat threads are on the left sidebar (you may have to open the sidebar). To find it on the app, you can go to the menu and select "History" to see your previous chats. These chats will be very important.

Each chat should have its own goal. Meaning, if you're looking to spice up grandma's old recipes with a Gordon Ramsey twist, keep that chat separate from your travel-related ones. In fact, I even like to keep different parts of my travel prepping in separate chats. Use one chat to plan a route for an RV trip, another to find good flights, and another to find the best travel destination for when the kids are out of school.

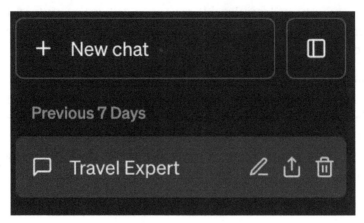

I recommend keeping track of these. You can do that by renaming each chat to something you can remember. As of today, you can click the pencil button next to the chat on the desktop version or when you go into history on your phone app, hold the chat you want to rename for 3 seconds, and a prompt to delete or rename will pop up. No need to get clever with the chat names. Something clear, like "road trip to Montana routes" should be enough to keep your AI planning organized.

The Priming

ChatGPT, you are a travel expert specializing in planning vacations for a couple that loves eating in restaurants and walking around a city in NON Schengen Europe or African. Your task is to help me find a city I can summer in with a budget of under 2000. I love walking and taking subways and taking trains through cities and bustling beaches with a lots of restaurants, stunning landscapes, or things to do and trying out local cuisines at mid-range restaurants. I prefer staying in boutique hotels, serviced apartments, and vacation rentals, etc. and using public transportation or walking, etc. to explore the cities or beaches. The cities you suggest should have mild weather, with temperatures ranging between 40 and 83 Fahrenheit during my stay. consider how long a US citizen can stay without needing a visa or with a visa upon arrival. In a minute, I will ask you to suggest a bulleted list that includes the countries I should visit along with recommended cities to stay for a month or more along with the pros and cons of each place. MAKE SURE TO AVOID SCHENGEN ZONE COUNTRIES. Before we get started, do you have any questions for me so you can best understand my needs?

Priming is one of the secret sauces for using AI. This will help clarify the goal of the AI and help ChatGPT give you the best results possible. Priming is essentially telling ChatGPT what it is and what you want from it.

Let me give you an example.

"ChatGPT, you are an experienced travel agent who specializes in planning memorable trips for families. You have a lot of experience finding mid-range budget accommodations, with plenty of unique activities to do nearby."

Ninja Tip- Level up Your Priming

Ending with a question can significantly level up both your priming and prompts. Get into the habit of ending with "Do you understand?" at the end of most priming and prompts.

I highly recommend you take your priming to another level by having ChatGPT ask *you* questions. It may take a few extra minutes, but the results will be so much better.

"In a minute, I am going to ask you to recommend a list of countries to travel to in the summer with a family of four traveling with two kids under the age of 8. Before I do so, what questions do you have for me?"

You're probably going to be surprised by how much the AI asks you. Take your time answering them with as many details as possible and end with *"Do you have any other questions for me?"* until your AI confirms it has enough information.

Problems?

I was once working on a packing list. I had primed it long ago and wanted a packing list. It started generating a packing list for a road trip in my car. At first, I was confused. I later realized I was on a chat thread I had primed to find the best road trip route. Don't forget to make sure you're in the right thread before getting started.

Priming & Prompts Examples

Don't worry about taking notes. Again, you can have a PDF of all my handiest travel prompts, and more, emailed over to you. Visit RobotsDoStuff.com and tell me where to send the list.

Chapter Five

ChatGPT for the Prissy ...and Others

How to Write Killer Prompts

I'm not sure if I am prissy or overly picky... or simply unafraid to ask for what I want, but when I am choosing my next place to stay, I have a lot of preferences I like to keep in mind. As a digital nomad, I need to have reliable internet. After my stay in a place that is hot, I want the weather to be beautiful. I also enjoy moderate to large-sized cities with modern conveniences and restaurant options.

A lot... I know.

Normally, this means a ton of Googling and scouring through blog posts, but now, I use ChatGPT to do the research for me.

The key is to give ChatGPT a great prompt.

In short, a prompt is telling ChatGPT what you want. But... the more vague you are, the more likely you are going to get a crap response. Better priming and prompting leads to better results.

Give Detail

The more specific you are, the better. Instead of saying, "*I want to plan a trip*," say, "*I want to plan a two-week family vacation to Japan in July, focusing on cultural experiences and kid-friendly activities.*"

Give Context

Providing context helps ChatGPT better understand your needs. For example, "*Considering I love hiking and photography, what are some must-visit spots in the Rocky Mountains?*"

Note What Format You're Looking For

Specify the format of the response you're looking for. Do you want a list of destinations? A detailed itinerary? A quick yes or no answer? Let ChatGPT know.

Preferences

Don't shy away from sharing your preferences. Love boutique hotels? Hate long flights? The more ChatGPT knows about your likes and dislikes, the better it can tailor its responses to you.

Put it Together

Put it all together and you get a considerably better prompt.

"In a minute, I am going to ask you to generate a detailed, bulleted list of the best picturesque countries in Europe to visit for two weeks with a family with kids under 8 in June, July, or August. I prefer countries with mild weather and beaches with plenty of water activities. Do you understand? Before answering, are there questions you have for me so you can deliver the best answer?"

Ask One Question at a Time

Traveling has a lot of parts to it. Tackle one travel goal at a time. Narrow down what country you're going to visit BEFORE asking for a list of accommodations.

Avoid saying something like *"I want you to help me plan a trip to Europe. Generate a list of countries with mild weather in the summer and a list of the best hotels to stay near the water."* Instead, consider splitting that into three different chats: one for finding the best country, one for finding the best city, and one for finding the best accommodations.

Finally, Be Patient

I know. Gross.

I hate being patient as well, but patience pays off with AI. When ChatGPT goes rogue, and trust me, it probably will, you can either gently prompt it back to your goal (*"don't forget I was looking for countries with mild weather"*), ask ChatGPT if it understands or is confused, or simply start a new chat. If you start a new chat, you can copy your original prime prompt to save a little time.

Sometimes, ChatGPT gets off track and it's not worth the hassle trying to correct the ship. Either way, learning to use When you learn how to use it, AI can save a lot of time compared to Googling.

Chapter Six

So, How Much Does Stuff Cost?

Creating a Travel Budget

T ravel budgeting... is a weirdly complex topic to write about. I didn't realize it until I started writing this chapter. In fact, with budgeting, I find there are more or less three camps of people.

- **Camp A**: They know their budget. For some people, their budget is what their budget is. They only have X amount to spend on their vacation — not a penny more. Or, they both know what stuff costs and are so good with budgeting they can save virtually any amount of money (within reason) for traveling. If that's you, my friend, keep on trucking. No need to read this chapter.

- **Camp B**: They know their dream vacation, but not their budget. If that's you, you might be daydreaming about a luxurious honeymoon in Bora Bora or an epic girls' trip to Las Vegas, but you're not sure how much it costs.

- **Camp C**: They're not sure about their vacation or their budget. If this is you, you may not travel much and do not know what to save to travel. You probably have been wanting to travel more, but don't know where to start.

If you're in Camp B or Camp C, this is the chapter for you.

My Camp Bs, I want your vacation to be as epic as you imagined. But... before we start planning, how cemented in is this dream? Are you dreaming of Bora Bora specifically? Or will any beautiful water villa over clear water do? I ask because there are a lot of lesser-known islands that are just as stunning but less than half the price...

Ask yourself, what about this dream vacation makes it dreamlike? What about it is a non-negotiable? If it's seeing the Colosseum, that makes it easy. There's only one real Colosseum, but if your non-negotiable is being served fruity drinks with an umbrella on a white sandy beach with clear water, there are a lot of options. Like... a lot.

I had a friend ask if I thought $10,000 would be enough for him to vacation in Paris. I mean... if you WANT to spend that much in Paris, you certainly can... but you can also have an incredible, unforgettable experience for less than a third of that.

Where to start?

The key to creating a good travel budget is creating one that meets your travel goals. For that, you need to know what those travel goals are. For those of you who know what vacation you are saving for, great, let's plug the info into ChatGPT and figure out how much it will cost.

If you don't know exactly what vacation you'll be going on, you can use a travel template to help you make a budget.

Let me explain.

Make a Travel Template

Before I made the switch to full-time travel, I knew travel had to be a part of my life. It was an absolute must for my mental health. At the time, I was working painfully boring corporate jobs and needed something to look forward to. I wanted to do at least one big vacation and a few smaller trips to tide me over. I created a "template" for the type of travel I wanted to do.

My "Small" Trip Template: My, now husband, and I, want to travel alone or with friends for 3-4 days, within the States, staying in midrange hotels, in a walkable area, 0-3 miles from attractions, surrounded by lots of activities.

My "Big, Once-a-Year" Trip Template: We want to go on a 7-10 day trip abroad. It would be a beach vacation, ideally, all-inclusive, with 2-3 excursions, with 2-4 friends or close family joining.

To me, traveling with friends was so much fun. I wanted them to be a part of my travel experience. You may disagree... To make your own travel template, ask yourself the following questions:

1. Destination Type: Do you prefer a beach destination, city exploration, mountain retreat, cultural immersion, or any specific type of place you want to visit?

2. Travel Dates: What are your preferred travel dates or the time of the year you plan to travel? (Seasonal variations can impact costs.)

3. Trip Duration: How long do you intend to stay at the destination?

4. Accommodation Preference: Are you looking for luxury hotels, budget-friendly hostels, or something in between?

5. Transportation: Do you plan to travel by air, train, car, or a combination? Will you need local transportation at the destination?

6. Activities & Interests: What activities and experiences are a must for your trip? (e.g., adventure sports, cultural tours, spa retreats, culinary experiences, etc.)

7. Dining Style: Do you prefer fine dining experiences, or are you open to exploring local eateries and street food?

8. Travel Companions: How many people will travel with you? Will you be sharing expenses with them? Sometimes, this doesn't matter if you are planning on everyone getting their own hotel, however, if you're planning on an Airbnb, this can be important.

9. Travel Insurance: Do you plan to purchase travel insurance for the trip? Note: Some credit cards will provide some travel insurance coverage. If you want a list of the top travel credit cards, go to RobotsDoStuff.com.

10. Currency & Conversion: Some currencies, like the UK's British Pound, are strong against the dollar. Keep that in mind when researching the cost of activities, dining, etc.

11. Emergency Fund: Are you setting aside a separate amount for unforeseen expenses or emergencies during the trip?

If you don't know the answer to all of these questions, that's fine, but answer them as completely as you can. The more info you have now, the more accurately you can create a budget for your trip. If you find yourself unable to select between a beach vacation, going to a historic destination, or taking a cruise, note all three and use ChatGPT to generate a budget for all three. You may find they are similarly priced and budgeting may not be an issue. If they are very different, it may help you make a decision about the travel type, or if you are still uncertain, you can simply save for the most expensive trip option.

ChatGPT to Find Your Travel Budget

Once you know your vacation or vacation template, you can use ChatGPT to create a travel budget estimate for you. You can do that by first priming your chat if you haven't already.

The Priming

"You are a travel expert and detail-oriented travel advisor. Do you understand?"

The Prompt

Now, prompt ChatGPT to give you a good budget.

"In a minute, I am going to ask you to create a detailed budget estimation for an upcoming vacation. I want to know both the estimated breakdown of what I'll be spending money on and the total expected cost for the trip. I am traveling to (insert your vacation plans) [OR: I am not sure exactly where I am traveling, but I can tell you the type of vacation I want]. Before moving forward, I want to feed you my travel preferences. Are you ready?

If you want to do multiple trips per year, like I wanted to, I recommend doing each trip type one at a time. After you have fed ChatGPT your travel preferences, add this prompt:

"Do you understand my travel preferences? Do you have any additional questions to give me the best possible travel advice and budget recommendations?"

If ChatGPT asks you questions, answer them as detailed as you can. Don't be afraid to admit you don't know something yet. You can say something like, *"I don't know that yet. I think I will want [to stay in a beach resort, a safe country outside of the US, etc.]."*

When answering ChatGPT's questions, try not to hit the ENTER key in between each question. If you do and it submits it before you are complete, you can hit "stop generating" if ChatGPT is replying to you and either finish answering all the questions or go to the last message you wrote, edit your response, and resubmit it.

Now that you have answered the questions, you can ask it for your budget:

"In a minute, I am going to ask you to create a detailed budget estimation for an upcoming vacation. I want to know both the estimated breakdown of what I'll be spending money on and the total expected cost for the trip/type of trip I want to take. Using the preferences I fed you, generate a detailed bullet list of all expected costs. Give me a budget range for each bullet list item. At the end of each bulleted item, give me a total estimated cost. Do you understand? Do you have any questions for me?"

Repeat this for each vacation/vacation type you want to do each year. Combine the costs and you have your travel savings goal. If that number knocked you out of your socks, read the upcoming chapter about stretching your money during your travels to see how that number could go down without you sacrificing too much, if any, quality. Sometimes a simple tweak like changing the season in which you travel can make a HUGE difference in how much you're going to spend. If you don't believe me, look up flights from Phoenix to Cancun on Dec. 22 and again on Jan. 22.

Chapter Seven

Budget as I Say... Not as I Do...

How to Stick to a Budget

I feel like a bit of a hypocrite writing a chapter on budgeting but I actually have quite a lot of useful things to say on the subject... even if I *cough* could do better with applying it in my life *cough* *cough*.

Now that you know how much your travels are, we should create a budget. First off, if you're not "good at budgeting" don't beat yourself up. You're certainly not alone. For me, because I am a freelancer with a rollercoaster-like income, it can be even more challenging. I recommend making it super simple.

Practical Budgeting: Keep Your Budget Simple

Micro managing my spending makes me mental, and as a realist, I know I will not keep up with it. Instead of painstakingly tracking all of my spending, I estimated the low-end amount I expected to earn in a month and added up my reoccurring bills. Using this, I subtracted what I wanted to put into savings and divided the rest into 31 days.

I created what I call My Daily Spend Amount. Now, I have something simple to focus on.

Let's say My Daily Spend Amount is $50. If I spend $35 today, I could either "roll" the $15 into the next day or, better, "forget about it". If I have a few "forget about it days" or made more than the minimum expected earnings, at the end of the month, I would have a little extra money. That money could either go into savings or go towards a special outing or mini-trip.

For me, making sure I spend less than My Daily Spend Amount made it a TON easier to stay on track of my budget. I didn't have to link credit cards or input everything I purchased every month.

Tools to help

But, there are many people who don't want to go the route I went. Many of my friends feel that way. To them, keeping things simple means using a user-friendly tool or app to keep them on track. If that's you, I've listed some helpful and popular ones here but, again, no need to take notes. I will list these tools on my resources page: RobotsDoStuff.com.

Budget & Tracking:

Even though I don't prefer it, I know many people who are obsessed with a budgeting and money tracker app. My friend really loves Dave Ramsey's Every Dollar app for tracking purchases. There is a free version that requires you to manually add your purchases, which she likes because it holds her accountable for her purchases, or you can pay for an upgrade and auto-track purchases in linked accounts.

Easy Saving Tools:

Consider an auto-saving tool to pad your travel funds. Something like Acorn's Round Up tool can help you by rounding purchases to the nearest dollar and saving the change.

Rakuten or iBotta will give you rebates on the stuff you buy. Be careful with these. They can inspire overspending. The idea is to get rebates on things you already spend money on.

Use Points:

If you won't go wild on the spending, I recommend looking into "travel hacking". Swap your debit or cash payments with a credit card with points.

Wait until there is a signup bonus before getting a new points credit card. Typically, the signup bonus is enough to cover 1-2 flights or accommodations for a short trip. Usually, the signup bonus is contingent upon you spending a certain amount within a set period of time. Look out for that. I usually like to align my credit card sign-ups with any big purchases I am planning. Right before Christmas or when buying plane tickets are great times to get a new card. In fact, many travel cards will give you double or triple points for using your card on travel-related purchases.

Chapter Eight

How to Stretch Your Money Traveling

(Without Taking Boring Vacations)

I mentioned earlier this will be a "how-to" book covering two major things: how to travel better & longer and how to use AI to plan your travels.

This chapter is all about learning to travel better. I first want to address a few travel myths before diving in.

Fact: You don't have to spend an arm and a leg to travel.
Fact: Spending more on a vacation does not mean you'll like it more.
Fact: You can still have an amazing vacation staying like a local.
Fact: You can save a TON of money by tweaking a few things about your travel mindset.

Consider Budget Travel at Least For a While

Nope. Budget travel does NOT have to be staying in hostels... I mean... it can be if that's what you're into. I've stayed in some hostels that were AWESOME, but that's not what I am going to talk about here.

Matthew Kepnes' blog, Nomadicmatt.com, and book, *How to Travel the World on $50 a Day,* are still some of the best budget travel resources out there.

Follow budget travelers

I love following budget travelers on social media because new tools and web-sites come out all the time. As I learned about a new resource, I link to it in the travel journal notebook I created in the DayOne Journal app or in my Apple Notes.

Attractions

Being closer to attractions is more expensive for nearly everything you do: taxis, restaurants, shopping, and accommodations. Staying further away will have some transportation costs but food and shopping will often be half as expensive (and usually higher quality). I like to split the difference and either stay near lesser-known attractions or in the neighborhoods next to the areas with the attractions. It's usually still a walkable distance away or a cheap cab/subway ride away.

In Rome, we stayed across from a mind-blowingly beautiful church, called Basilica Papale di Santa Maria Maggiore, a large park, and tons of incredible restaurants and shops for an affordable price, because it wasn't inside the historic city center. But... it wasn't as "romantic" as staying in a hotel with a view of the Colosseum like during a previous trip had been.

Accommodations

If you can stay longer, you can enjoy some impressive discounts. I like to stay 1-2 months per apartment, because shorter stays equate to higher costs, both in transportation costs and in higher costing accommodations. Airbnb will give huge discounts if you stay for 2 weeks and an even bigger discount if you stay for a month or more.

More companies are catching on. Most Americans forget that there are more accommodation sites than Airbnb, Booking.com, Expedia, etc., which are popular ones in the USA, but less so abroad. Agota is big in Asia. DNAstay, Trawerk, and GoingRemotely are big in Croatia. You can even find luxury, serviced apartments in Hanoi on websites such as ServicedApartmentsinHanoi.com.

To find these websites, I do a search for something like "affordable, short-term apartments + city" or "luxury, serviced apartments + city" on Google.

I also follow blogs and vlogs on YouTube. I have a few "go to" places I will check for info on a city or country. My favorite is NomadicMatt.com, but another is Nomadlist.com. The latter will give you a general rating of a city based on things like cost of living, fun, safety, "good for families", etc. They have a community chat where you can ask people for housing recommendations for the city you are looking for.

Social media is a pretty good resource. I will follow a quality travel influencer on Instagram, but I will also search for Facebook groups for travelers visiting a country or city as well as groups for short-term rentals in that same city/country. If you are staying for 1-3+ months, you can link with realtors on Messenger.

Pro Tip: Be polite, patient, and follow up. Customer service is not the same abroad as it is in the USA. Gentle follow-ups are best. I was impatient and missed out on some great deals for accommodations in Ho Chi Minh City.

Be wary of scams, however. Facebook group members are vocal about anyone who is a scam, so read through some of those posts and don't be afraid to ask questions about where the best place to stay is and any recommended real estate agents.

Time of year

Travel in off-seasons for the country. Most of Europe's off-season is during winter, fall, and early spring. In Asia, their off-season is during the rainy season. Summer is usually more expensive nearly everywhere in the world. That's because everyone's kids are out of school more or less around the same time. If you can swing it, try to travel any other time of year (avoiding holidays).

I don't want you to have a bad experience. Please, please, please do a bit of research on how a place is during the time you are considering. Be honest about your own preferences! If you hate rain and an unexpected thunderstorm would ruin your vacation, travel to Bali during the busy season instead of during their rainy, off-season.

But, if a couple hours of rain is well worth the half-priced luxury hotel stay, let it rain, baby!

Remember, if you only get 2 weeks off a year, and you don't want to deal with rain on your few precious vacation days a year, be completely honest. You're not being a diva, you're being kind to yourself. I want you to have great travel experiences. That means you'll need to be real with yourself about what brings you joy.

Use points

I briefly mentioned this earlier, but it's worth noting here. There are amazing credit cards out there that allow you to earn points toward travel (and more). I recommend waiting until they have an amazing sign-up bonus. I opt for cards that have no foreign transaction fees, lounge access, and plenty of travel-related perks. My Sapphire Chase Card has a high annual fee but provides travel insurance that ends up saving me money, even considering the $700-ish dollars I pay towards the annual fee.

Most credit cards will run specials where they give extra points to incentivize using certain brands. Typically, it doesn't cost more to use these brands, but it earns you more points, which can save on accommodations, flights, rental cars, or upgrades.

Summary

If you can follow these principles... and plug them into your ChatGPT prompts, ChatGPT should be able to find smoking deals.

Chapter Nine

The Hunt For My Summer Paradise

Finding Your Next Country

I fully understand most of you will not struggle to find the country you want to visit next. You probably have a small list of countries and cities you want to visit. If this is you, great! Skip the next couple of chapters.

But, for me, this was an odd "challenge" I ran into. So, because of that, I added the next couple of chapters to the book to show you how I figured it out.

I had made my way to Da Nang, Vietnam, almost by accident. Vietnam had not been on my radar as a top travel destination, but I found a stunning place on Airbnb that was stupidly inexpensive.

We made our way from Bangkok to Da Nang with me doing the least amount of research on a country I've ever done in my life. I researched COVID travel requirements (we went there in 2023 after most countries had done away with requirements, but we wanted to make sure) and visa requirements, but nothing about what the city was like.

No surprise, it was hot. Nearly all of Asia was during the time I visited, but other than that, I was in love. Da Nang was a complete surprise: white sandy beach, beautiful water, a big, bustling city, plenty of conveniences, and unbelievable prices.

But, eventually, the heat got to me and I was craving cooler weather. When I started looking for where to travel next summer, I ran into some issues. I hadn't realized how many preferences I had collected during my travels as a digital nomad. Meaning, to qualify as a great place to visit next summer, I had a lot of requirements for it to meet. Call me prissy, but that is one bonus being a nomad affords me. I can be picky because I can go anywhere in the world. ...well, that I can afford to travel to...

You can do the same with your vacations!

Don't get me wrong, if a place has a good amount of the things I am looking for, I will still visit, but the fun thing about asking for exactly what I want is actually finding it! The world is HUGE. The more I travel, the more I realize how little I actually know about it.

So, I gave ChatGPT a challenge. It responded imperfectly but, with a little guidance, it pulled through and found me a place I had never heard about, but on paper, meets every little demand I had!

Let me walk you through how I discovered Mauritius, a stunningly beautiful island with strong internet and gorgeous August weather off the coast of East Africa.

A little background

We already had plans to be in Europe. A good amount of Western Europe is inside what is called the Schengen Region. For those of you who don't know, US citizens can travel within this zone for 90 days within a 180-day period. Meaning, on day 91, we must be out of the ENTIRE zone. So, that dramatically limits our Europe travel.

My husband and I were looking for a country to spend the summer that wasn't too far away from Italy, where we wanted to return after our 120-day Schengen time relapsed and we could return. But, of course, also wouldn't be hot, had strong enough internet, and would be a big enough city to keep me happy for 2-3 months. The challenge was on. Time to see if ChatGPT was up to the task.

The Priming

"ChatGPT, you are an expert travel agent. You specialize in working with Digital Nomads looking for places to stay for a few months. Do you understand?"

The Prompt

"Great. I am looking for a place to stay during the month of August in non-Schengen Europe, the eastern part of the Middle East, or Africa that has weather between 40 degrees Fahrenheit and 84 degrees Fahrenheit, has plenty of restaurants and activities, fits in my budget of $2000/month, and has strong internet. Please generate a detailed bulleted list of 10-15 countries meeting these criteria, given the constraints. Before moving forward, are there any questions you have for me?"

The Mistake

Great! Based on your preferences, here is a list of cities outside the Schengen Zone in Europe and Africa that you could consider for your summer vacation. Each city comes with its pros and cons, taking into account your interests, budget, mild weather, and visa requirements:

1. Lisbon, Portugal:
   * Pros: Beautiful architecture, vibrant food scene, mild weather during summer, bustling beaches, and rich historical sites.
   * Cons: Can be crowded during peak tourist season.
2. Split, Croatia:
   * Pros: Stunning coastal city, historic old town, delicious local cuisine, moderate summer temperatures, and easy access to nearby islands.
   * Cons: Can be crowded with tourists, especially in popular areas.
3. Marrakech, Morocco:
   * Pros: Exotic atmosphere, vibrant markets, unique Moroccan cuisine, fascinating historical sites (such as the Medina), warm summer weather, and beautiful landscapes.
   * Cons: High temperatures in summer (can exceed 83°F), potential language barrier.
4. Istanbul, Turkey:
   * Pros: Rich history, magnificent architecture (including the Hagia Sophia and Blue Mosque), diverse culinary scene, pleasant summer weather, and a vibrant atmosphere.
   * Cons: Can be crowded, potential language barrier.
5. Cape Town, South Africa:
   * Pros: Breathtaking landscapes (Table Mountain, Cape Peninsula), diverse cuisine, pleasant summer temperatures, beautiful beaches, and a vibrant cultural scene.
   * Cons: Longer travel distance, potential visa requirements for US citizens (check visa regulations beforehand).
6. Casablanca, Morocco:
   * Pros: Cosmopolitan city, blend of modern and traditional architecture, delicious Moroccan cuisine, mild summer weather, and proximity to beautiful beaches.
   * Cons: Less historical sites compared to other cities on the list.

Remember to check visa requirements for each specific destination as they can vary for US citizens. Additionally, consider the COVID-19 situation and any travel restrictions or entry requirements that may be in place at the time of your trip.

ChatGPT asked me a few questions. I answered as thoroughly as I could, and it started generating a list. Already, I saw a couple of mistakes. One country on the list I knew to be part of the Schengen Region and another I knew to be boiling in the summer. If you don't know right off the bat if there is a mistake on a list generated for you, when ChatGPT gives you a list, read through the details and pick a few favorites and fact-check those.

The Correction

Since I knew ChatGPT had given me a couple of mistakes, I went ahead and re-prompted it to give me a whole new list.

"Some countries do not match all of my criteria. Please remember to generate a list of countries NOT part of the Schengen region, have mild weather in August (not greater than 85 degrees Fahrenheit), have plenty of restaurants and activities, fit in my budget of $2000, and have strong internet."

Now, I have a much better list. There were several countries I had expected. I knew the UK would be on there because there are some cities we could stretch our budget, but as the dollar was much weaker than the pound, I wanted to find a different option. I had learned that when a country barely fit within our budget, I was less happy with the accommodation options I could afford. Since I had never heard of Mauritius, I googled it and fact-checked all of my specifications. I was thrilled when I found it suited our needs!

Chapter Ten

Tiny Towns & Other Woes

Finding Your Next City

I t's no secret finding the right city to stay in your travels can make or break the trip. But finding the best place to stay isn't always as straightforward as it seems. Yes, if you want to visit Rome one day, the city is kinda already picked for you, but... if you want "to visit Italy" one day, that puts you in a different situation. One city vs another makes an enormous difference in Italy.

Ask yourself what your goals are. Yes, that is a thing... Think about it. If you are a busy parent, stretched thin and you're finally getting away with your spouse, the goal probably should be to relax and focus on romance as opposed to sprinting all over a busy, bustling city — unless that's your thing.

The biggest reason people need a vacation right after they've had a vacation is because they do too much when they should be recovering. (...and I suppose because it's hard to go back to work after taking time off...) Hey, if that doesn't appeal to you, don't take my advice, but that is kinda the point of what I am saying... You should ask *yourself* what you want out of this trip. Do you need some serious romance and recovery? ...or do you need to explore? Do you want to experience different cultures and see history? ...or do you need to gorge yourself on delicious food and wine next to a stunning coastline?

Also, consider how long your vacation is. If you're trying to run and explore and *Go! Go! Go!* for two weeks straight, don't be surprised if you're sick when you finally drag your exhausted self onto the flight home. I want to help people explore more, easier, and have a better experience doing it. I want you to love travel — crave it, even. Seriously asking yourself *"What do I want?"* is weirdly a rare question these days.

I personally like to switch it up — do a blend of both. If my travel is longer than a week, relaxing the whole time would bore me. I need a little exploration mixed in. There are two stunningly beautiful places I made this mistake in: San Juan del Sur, Nicaragua and Cefalu, Sicily, Italy. Both are idyllic places. They are small, romantic, and picturesque. Some of the most beautiful beach sunsets were in that small town in Nicaragua. Because we were meeting friends there (something kinda rare during full-time travel), we stayed for 2 months.

For me, it was a huge mistake. I was bored to tears within 3 weeks. I had tried nearly every restaurant in our small town and even the grocery stores were tiny. The bars, though beautiful and perfectly located, would water down their drinks, so if I wasn't in the mood for beer, going out wasn't a good option. It bore me to go on walks along the coastline, something which had previously been the greatest activity ever, only a few weeks before.

Something similar happened with Cefalu, a stunningly beautiful Italian town slightly larger than the tiny San Juan del Sur. I loved everything about it... until I was over it and counting the days until I could leave. Had I been to both cities for a few weeks, you wouldn't be able to shut me up about how great the trip was, but because we stayed longer, I was going out of my mind.

Being honest about what you need for the duration of your trip is key. If you want an amazing experience, maybe wait until you are rested and energetic enough to do a big city like Rome, or split your time between Rome and a romantic beach place like Positano. If you're feeling a bit estranged from your spouse or partner, maybe opt for Nice instead of Paris.

Keep this in mind when you're telling AI what you want. "I need relaxation and romance." "I want to connect with the local culture." "I want to learn about history." Tell your AI what your goals are out of this trip and you'll get a vacation that is memorable and fulfilling.

Following my Mauritius example, I had found a country I wanted to stay for the month of August for a few months, but I didn't know where in Mauritius would be best. So using ChatGPT, I found my next city

The Priming

"ChatGPT, you are a travel expert who specializes in finding the best spots for digital nomads to stay for one to three months. Do you understand?"

If you're in the same chat, you don't have to prime it again unless you want it to take other things into consideration, like if I wanted to take a break from work and needed a honeymoon-like vacation instead of a spot suitable for a digital nomad.

The Prompt

"I want you to find the best city for me to stay for one to three months as a digital nomad on the island of Mauritius. I need to have plenty to do. I love having restaurants and shops and activities within walking distance of my place. I love a city that is walkable. My budget is $2,000 a month or less. I need strong internet and I want to be close to the beach. The weather needs to be under 85 degrees Fahrenheit in August. Please generate a detailed list of cities you would recommend."

Based on these search criteria, I found the country's capital fit well with my specifications. I took my favorite from the list and I did a little internet sleuthing to make sure it fit. I looked at YouTube videos and images on Google Maps and tried to gauge the size of the city. After, I Googled the internet speed as well to make sure I had found a suitable location.

The search took about 15 minutes versus the 2+ hours it usually takes to find my next vacation.

Big win.

Chapter Eleven

The Swamp Crotch Shuffle

Choosing When to Visit

I was glaring at the tiny air-conditioning unit doing absolutely nothing. It was August. We were in the Vatican Museum, and I was furious. I was shuffling my feet forward because there were too many people to take a full step. Sweat had just dripped down my butt crack and I was counting down the seconds until I could get out of the museum I had dropped $34 a person to be inside of.

I was big mad...and confused. Five years before, I had been in this same place, mesmerized by the talented artists featured inside the massive, maze-like building. But that boiling August day, I just couldn't get over how hot and crowded it was, let alone appreciate the art. August and November presented totally different Romes and I can tell you unequivocally which I prefer.

Deciding when to visit can really and truly make or break your trip. Some of you will not have much of a choice for a while. If you have kids and insane work hours, your travel time is your travel time. Please don't use it as an excuse not to travel! But, unless you can ignore the crowds and don't mind having swamp crotch, I recommend prioritizing visiting places that are lovely in the summer. Seriously, I would hate for you to despise Rome. It's a magical place ... in the fall and winter.

AI can help you find beautiful places to visit during the time you have to travel, and if you have flexibility, it can help you match your ideal travel cities with the best time of year to visit. You can avoid crowds, extreme weather, price hikes, and more. Some of these matches might surprise you. In fact, many travel influencers love Bali during the rainy season. Though it can have crazy downpours, the rain usually lasts less than a couple of hours, but the crowds are close to zero and the rates are significantly lower. Up to you if the tradeoff of thunderstorms is worth it, but to me, I fully intend to visit in the future during the rainy season!

If you only have one time of the year to travel, obviously, this chapter is of no use to you. Feel free to skip it. I certainly don't want you to skip traveling because you can only travel one time a year.

That being said, please, please, please keep in mind some places are going to be less pleasant to visit during the summertime. So if you're like me and don't want to have a bad experience in a spot only because of the weather, either work hard to keep an open mind or save that destination for future travels when your traveling can be a little more flexible.

If you can be flexible, whether that means you have access to a babysitter or can steal the kids away from their school for a once-a-year trip, definitely take advantage of this chapter. Flexibility can be the biggest secret as far as finding great deals, as I mentioned earlier.

Now, some things are self-explanatory. The Northern Lights, for example, only happen at a certain time of year. So if that's your goal, that's a great time to go. But if you are trying to see Finland for more than the Northern Lights, going when they're happening, can be a much more expensive and crowded time to travel.

A good example is October Fest. October Fest can be a wonderful experience, but probably not the best time to visit Germany. If you really want to see the "real" Germany, come at a different time of year. October Fest is fun, but if you are not taking part in the heavy, heavy drinking every night you're there, it can be a little exhausting and rowdy, especially if you're trying to do a trip with the family.

If you can:

Be Flexible: If possible, try to be flexible with your travel dates. AI might suggest a time you hadn't considered but could offer better weather, fewer crowds, or lower prices.

Consider Your Interests: Are you a foodie who wants to experience a city's culinary scene? ...or maybe you're an adventurer who's into hiking and outdoor activities? Include these details in your prompt. The best time to visit a place can vary depending on your interests.

I want to visit India. I don't think it's going to happen for a couple of years, unfortunately, but when it does, I want it to be a wonderful experience. Let's use ChatGPT to find out the best time to travel to India.

Let's experiment.

The Priming

"You are an excellent, experienced travel advisor who knows all about traveling to India. Do you understand?"

The Prompt

"I'm interested in going on a three-month trip to India. Within this time, I'm going to spend one month in each of the following cities: Mumbai, New Delhi, and Goa. I wanted to have mild weather, with little to no rain. Generate a list of the best months to visit with the pros and cons and details."

The Response

Mumbai:

Best Months to Visit: November to February

Pros:

- *Pleasant weather with mild temperatures ranging from 15˚C to 25˚C*

(59 °F to 77 °F).

- *Festive atmosphere due to various cultural celebrations and events during this time.*

- *Ideal for outdoor activities, sightseeing, and exploring the city.*

Cons:

- *Crowds might still be present due to the holiday season.*

- *Higher accommodation prices compared to other times of the year.*

- *Nights can get slightly chilly, so bring some light warm clothing.*

New Delhi:

Best Months to Visit: October to March

Pros:

- *Pleasant and comfortable weather with temperatures ranging from 10 °C to 25 °C (50 °F to 77 °F).*

- *Major festivals like Diwali and Holi fall during this period, providing cultural experiences.*

- *Ideal for sightseeing, historical explorations, and outdoor activities.*

Cons:

- *November to January can see some fog and smog, affecting visibility.*

- *The peak tourist season can result in moderately crowded tourist spots.*

- *December and January might have cooler nights, so carrying a light jacket is advisable.*

Goa:

Best Months to Visit: November to February

Pros:

- *Dry and comfortable climate with temperatures ranging from 20 °C to 30 °C (68 °F to 86 °F).*

- *Festive and lively atmosphere due to Christmas and New Year celebrations.*

- *Ideal for beach activities, water sports, and relaxation.*

Cons:

- *Higher number of tourists during Christmas and New Year can lead to slightly higher prices.*

- *Accommodation may fill up quickly, so booking in advance is recommended.*

- *Nights can get cooler, so packing a light sweater or jacket is a good idea.*

Now, that's what I call a helpful response! It's thorough, and I can decide if the cons are worth the benefits of visiting during these months.

Chapter Twelve
A Different Rome

Picking the Best Neighborhood

I was blinking back tears after having just been yelled at by a person asking for money.

I was walking to the Colosseum, trying to remember the dreamlike trip I had taken to this same city five years prior. Was this really the same romantic Roma or had it all been in my imagination?

Fast forward to today, I've actually had a wonderful experience in multiple neighborhoods within Rome, but I can say unequivocally that staying within the historical district makes a big difference. They designed the historical district with vacationers in mind. It is beautiful and romantic and breathtaking. It's also not what most Italians would call the "real" Rome.

Staying outside of the historical district was still beautiful, but it was far less intimate and romantic. ...but the food was significantly less expensive and tasted a lot better. They also spoke very little English, if any, and didn't understand what a tip was.

Outside of the historical center feels "lived in" and authentic. Buuuut if you're looking for romantic and dreamlike- it's not the place for you. Many vacationers, especially Americans who work long hours, week after week, want a trip that feels like a vacation. Adventures are for those without 9-5's, right? If you agree, keep this in mind when you're planning your trips. It might be worth the extra cost to stay in a place that feels like a wonderland.

Let's talk about how ChatGPT can help find the perfect neighborhood for you to stay in. Let's look at Bali.

Bali is not a very walkable place. By that, I mean it is very spread out, so where you stay can make a big impact on your experience. If you are "commuting" every day of your vacation, you may not like your trip as much as if you found the perfect spot to stay and explore.

The Priming

"ChatGPT, you are an expert traveler and travel advisor. You're well versed in traveling to Bali. Do you understand?

The Prompt

"Generate a bulleted list of the best neighborhoods for a couple traveling with 2 small children. Include descriptions of each area along with the pros and cons of staying in each area."

The Response

<u>**Sanur:**</u>
Description: Sanur is known for its family-friendly atmosphere and calm beaches. It offers a more relaxed and quieter ambiance compared to some other areas in Bali.

Pros:

- *Shallow and calm waters make it suitable for children to swim.*

- *Wide range of family-friendly accommodations.*

- *Beachside paths for cycling and strolling.*

Cons:

- *May have fewer nightlife and entertainment options compared to other areas.*

- *Limited shopping and dining choices compared to busier areas.*

Nusa Dua:
Description: Nusa Dua is a luxurious enclave with upscale resorts and a beautiful beach, making it ideal for a family seeking a more upscale and tranquil experience.

Pros:

- *Gorgeous and clean beaches with calm waters.*

- *High-end resorts with comprehensive facilities for families.*

- *Gated and secure environment.*

Cons:

- *Can be more expensive compared to other areas in Bali.*

- *Limited interaction with local culture and less vibrant street life.*

Seminyak:

Description: Seminyak offers a mix of trendy and family-friendly elements, making it suitable for a couple with children who want a balance of relaxation and entertainment.

Pros:

- *Beaches with great surf and stunning sunsets.*

- *Wide range of dining options, from casual to upscale.*

- *Boutiques and shops for shopping.*

Cons:

- *Can be crowded and bustling, which might not suit those seeking a quieter environment.*

- *Nightlife might not be suitable for young children.*

Canggu:

Description: Canggu combines a relaxed atmosphere with a growing number of family-friendly facilities, making it an emerging hotspot for travelers with kids.

Pros:

- *Beaches with a more laid-back vibe and good surf.*

- *More family-friendly cafes, restaurants, and activities.*

- *Opportunities for family-friendly yoga classes and outdoor adventures.*

Cons:

- *Infrastructure might be less developed compared to more established areas.*

- *Traffic congestion during peak hours.*

Ubud:

Description: Ubud offers a cultural and nature-focused experience, perfect for families interested in exploring Balinese traditions and the island's lush landscapes.

Pros:

- *Beautiful rice terraces and natural surroundings.*

- *Art markets, galleries, and cultural performances.*

- *Tranquil ambiance and cooler temperatures.*

Cons:

- *Limited beach access, as Ubud is located inland.*

- *Less emphasis on beach activities and water sports.*

I really love the list it generated. It's the perfect jumping-off spot for my research. Now, I can review the pros and cons, narrow down the list, and then Youtube a couple of my favorites before choosing my final destination.

Chapter Thirteen

A Tornado of Dogs

Finding the Perfect Accommodation

I found the perfect apartment in a great location...at least I thought it was perfect....

We were in Tbilisi, Georgia and moving into a bigger apartment because my in-laws were visiting. I found a beautiful apartment above a roundabout leading to a strip of bars and restaurants.

I am not a light sleeper, so I don't consider noise at night when choosing my accommodations. Occasionally, this bites me on the butt. This was one of those times. It was May and warming up. The apartment we were in didn't have A/C, so we left the windows open.

Mistake...

If you've never been to Tbilisi, there are a lot of stray dogs. They are happy and well taken care of, but they can be noisy. At 3 am, in addition to the tornado of dogs hanging out under our apartment, were people doing donuts in their cars, and some jerk who thought putting the music at the loudest possible decibel and at max base was a good idea. I found myself sympathizing with my light sleeper friends and wondering what was going through the person's mind who was blasting music from his parked car so late.

So... If you don't want to be doing that, read reviews and descriptions mentioning the "quiet neighborhood". Being close to attractions is great, but not if you can't sleep. Sometimes the neighborhoods next to popular ones are the best. They are where the locals stay. Those have been my favorite places to stay so far. I've read reviews complaining about "going down some alley" to find their apartment, but if they are in safe areas, those can be the best! It's away from the busy traffic, honking horns, drunk singers, and shouting vendors.

When you use ChatGPT to find accommodations, unless you're looking for some generalities, I highly recommend you upgrade ChatGPT to the pro version. Right now, it's $20 a month, which I think is well worth it.

Once you've upgraded, go to your desktop and open a new ChatGPT 4 thread. Select 1-2 plugins for accommodations and at least one for a search engine.

The Priming

"ChatGPT, you are an expert travel agent. You are particularly well-versed in finding budget accommodations both beautiful and unique. You specialize in finding the best accommodations for families in Bali. Do you understand?"

The Prompt

"Find me a list of accommodations perfect for a family of four with two small children traveling to Canggu, Bali. We'll be staying for two weeks and we would love to find a walkable location, close to the beach. Our budget is $1,500. We don't want a kitchen, but we want a pool, Wi-Fi, and a tv. We need at least two bedrooms and a living room area to hang out."

So what I've been doing is using ChatGPT to generate a list so I can kind of see what's out there as far as hotels go, and doing a comparative search through Airbnb for the same filters.

Chapter Fourteen

The Thousandaire's Dream Wedding

Finding Killer Flight Deals

When I told my friends and family I wanted to do my wedding in Italy, I was surprised by how many of them were so supportive.

In fact, many of my friends were relieved I made that decision. Before the announcement, I was getting frustrated. I was excited to be engaged, but when I had "planned" my wedding as a kid, I had assumed I would be a millionaire. (Dreams of kids, eh?) Now, my cliff-side wedding, overlooking the ocean seemed... improbable.

So, I did what every 30-year-old thousandaire would do. I adjusted my expectations. — Well, I tried to. I quickly learned that my adjusted budget of

$2500 was a bit of a fairytale. I knew I didn't want to do a courthouse wedding, but everything else was just too expensive. Out of nowhere, the idea to elope formed in my mind, and then, excited to combine my honeymoon and wedding, a new plan formed.

When I did my initial budgeting, I Googled how much a flight from Arizona to Rome was and it blew me away to see I could fly round-trip for just over $500. When I found out flights were so reasonable, I was disappointed with myself. I mean... why hadn't I been going to Europe every year as an adult? Granted, I found those flights in 2017, but flights are not too much more expensive if you're able to be a little flexible.

Dates

Usually, summer is going to be more expensive. If you can fly in the Fall or Spring, typically, you will find much less expensive flights.

Hubs

There are certain international hubs around the US in particular where prices are dramatically less, compared to flying from your local airport. It might be significantly cheaper to do a quick hop to one of those hubs to fly across the ocean if that's your goal. In my case, I often find great deals on a flight from Los Angeles to Rome.

By the way, be careful! Different cities have different airports. There are multiple airports in Dallas, Paris, Bangkok, etc. If you're doing a layover or a round-trip flight out of one of these cities, make sure the airport codes match or accommodate for the travel time in between airports.

Sometimes it is cheaper to fly into one airport and out of another airport in the same city. I highly recommend this if it's less expensive, but you don't want to go to the wrong airport, so pay close attention when you book. I went to the wrong airport in Paris and trust me... You do not want the stress! We barely made our flight that day...

Buy on a Holiday

If you search online on, or just after, a major holiday, many companies will run a Holiday Flash Deal. I found great deals booking flights for later the following year, that I found just after Christmas. Admittedly, I've seen fewer deals since COVID, but I suspect that this rule will apply again soon.

Smaller Airports

Google Flights does a pretty good job of considering all airports, but it might be worth double-checking if a state or country you are trying to visit has a small, lesser-known airport. Smaller airports usually have budget airlines with discounted prices.

Be warned, friend... a budget airline ticket doesn't *always* mean a cheaper ticket. I have seen some shady things flying budget. $80 bag fees on a $20 flight, for example... Plus, if the location isn't near where you are going, taking an additional train or taxi can add to the cost, so be sure to do some research when opting for this route.

Use Points

I briefly mentioned this earlier, but if you haven't already, swap your debit card with a credit card with points for your purchases. I won't go into too many details in this book because travel hacking is quite an in-depth topic, but many travelers get free or discounted accommodations and flights by using points.

Follow Bloggers & Influencers

Follow people who travel the way you do or want to travel. I follow on Instagram. While I enjoy mindless scrolling from time to time, I love learning about useful travel tips, so it's nice when they come on my feed.

In fact, that is how I learned about things like Zip Fly, a budget airline in Tokyo that is launching a full, lay-back chair that is far less than the typical business class or first class flight. If you can swing the $2200 to fly from LA to Tokyo (which is not much more than a normal flight on a different airline, by the way), then you can have a fully reclining seat for the long flight. Talk about affordable luxury! If you can't swing that, they offer $600 round-trip tickets for their standard chair, which is also a great deal...

When to Buy

As a general rule, I buy international flights (from the USA to abroad) 3-4 months away from my trip and a domestic flight 1-2 months away unless I find a good deal around a holiday.

Tools like Google Flight Predictions or Hopper Flight Predictions can help you choose when is best to book your flights but they are rarely foolproof. I like Google Flight's Price History feature which shows if a price I am seeing is high and what price I should hold out for.

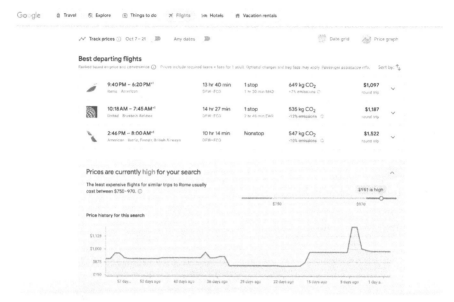

Again, the prices don't always go down. COVID did mess the travel industry up a bit, but in the last few months, it's seems like it's balancing back out.

I highly, highly, highly, highly recommend you use the Chrome Incognito Window. Unfortunately, a lot of travel sites will use cookies to ramp up prices when they think people are getting ready to buy. If you've ever researched flight prices and came back a day or two later and the price jumped 50 bucks, that's probably why. Incognito tabs help to hide your cookies from websites so the prices don't get ramped up just for you.

To do this, if you haven't already, download the Google Chrome browser for your computer, go to file, and open a new Incognito Window.

Where to Go

If you're flexible with where you want to go, Google Flights can be super handy in finding a unique travel destination for you.

I open a Google Chrome incognito tab, go to Google Flights, select Explore, enter your departure city, and enter the month I want to travel, but I'll leave the destination blank. Then, I open the map and hover over different countries (and states), looking at the prices. Maybe you're bored with visiting the same places over and over. This could inspire a whole new vacation destination!

Use ChatGPT to Do the Heavy Lifting for You

Typically, I only use ChatGPT when in the early stages of researching the cost of flights. This is because I can sometimes find better deals on Google Flights. I know other people who do things a bit differently, but that's personally my preference.

Here are some examples.

The Priming

First, open a new chat thread and select ChatGPT 4 (upgrade is required) with Travel plugins. I chose JetBook.Click, Expedia, and KeyMate.Ai. You can go to the plugin store and choose different ones if you wish. (Access the store by clicking on plugins and scrolling to the bottom. Google/YouTube it if you have trouble. Things may have changed since writing this book...)

"You are a travel expert who always finds the best deals on flights. You are great at finding seats right next to each other for couples and families. You're great at finding the best locations to fly in and out of, even if it's not in the same state, but in a neighboring state. You consider layovers and flight time. You also consider the quality of flights, taking into consideration reviews and safety standards. You are an expert travel agent and make recommendations even if I don't specifically request something. You are detailed in all of your responses and recommendations, and always give the pros and cons of the recommendations. Do you understand?"

Deciding Where to Fly to

The Prompt

"I live in Dallas and am looking to travel abroad. Generate a list of 10-15 airports in countries outside of the US that are inexpensive to fly from one of the airports in Dallas. I can fly any time in October. Please briefly describe the city and country the airport is located, along with a range of prices for round-trip economy flights. Do you understand?"

The Response

ChatGPT generated a list of 10 countries. I expected Mexico and a handful of South American countries, but ChatGPT actually surprised me with some countries I hadn't expected. I had no idea it was affordable to fly to the Caribbean, India, and the UAE!

Certainly! Here's a list of 10 international destinations you can fly to from Dallas in October, along with a brief description of the city and country, and a range of roundtrip economy flight prices:

1. **Cancun, Mexico** - A tropical beach paradise known for its beautiful beaches and vibrant nightlife.
   * **Price**: As low as $317 round trip.
2. **Mexico City, Mexico** - A bustling metropolis with a mix of historical monuments, modern architecture, world-class museums, and diverse cuisine.
   * **Price**: As low as $328 round trip.
3. **San Juan, Puerto Rico** - A Caribbean gem with a mix of beaches, colonial and Art Deco architecture in Old San Juan, and natural wonders.
   * **Price**: As low as $379 round trip.
4. **San Jose, Costa Rica** - A cultural hub with attractions like the National Theater and Pre-Columbian Gold Museum, and proximity to natural wonders.
   * **Price**: As low as $398 round trip.
5. **Charlotte Amalie, USVI** - A picturesque city with pastel houses, historical buildings, and Caribbean and Creole cuisine.
   * **Price**: As low as $427 round trip.
6. **San Salvador, El Salvador** - The country's transportation hub and gateway to sights like Coatepeque Caldera and El Boqueron National Park.
   * **Price**: As low as $477 round trip.
7. **Lima, Peru** - A city with a rich history, beautiful churches, and monasteries, and a gateway to the Andes.
   * **Price**: As low as $643 round trip.
8. **Shanghai, China** - A modern city with vibrant shopping districts, historical architecture, and cultural attractions.
   * **Price**: As low as $822 round trip.
9. **Mumbai, India** - An eclectic, cosmopolitan city with a mix of modern attractions and cultural heritage sites.
   * **Price**: As low as $822 round trip.
10. **Dubai, UAE** - A city of superlatives, known for its skyscrapers, luxury shopping, and cultural attractions.

* **Price**: As low as $853 round trip.

These prices are based on data and may vary depending on the time of booking, airline, and other factors. It's always a good idea to book in advance to secure the best deals. Safe travels! 🌐✈

Source

hopper.com

Deciding When to Fly

The Prompt

"I live in Dallas and am traveling to Brazil. I am flexible with when I can travel. What 3 months are the least expensive times to fly to this country?"

The Response

"Based on the search results, the least expensive months to fly from Dallas to Brazil are typically February, March, and November.

To Find Flights When You Know Where & When You Want to Travel

The Prompt

"I am looking for a flight. I live in Dallas, and I'm trying to take a vacation in Rome for 10 days. Where do you recommend I fly out of and how much will an economy flight round trip cost? Before you answer me, what questions do you have?"

The Response

After answering questions pertaining to travel dates, flexibility, layovers, and a couple more, ChatGPT responded with a list of flights.

Used JetBook.Click

Sure thing! Here are some flight options from Dallas to Rome:

Price	Flight	Departure	Arrival	Duration	Stopovers	Booking
$639	Turkish Airlines	Dallas (DFW) 2023-10-11 20:20	Rome (FCO) 2023-10-12 18:45	15h 25m	1	Click to book
$639	Turkish Airlines	Dallas (DFW) 2023-10-09 20:20	Rome (FCO) 2023-10-10 18:45	15h 25m	1	Click to book
$639	Turkish Airlines	Dallas (DFW) 2023-10-08 20:20	Rome (FCO) 2023-10-09 18:45	15h 25m	1	Click to book
$641	Turkish Airlines	Dallas (DFW) 2023-10-10 20:20	Rome (FCO) 2023-10-11 18:45	15h 25m	1	Click to book
$651	Turkish Airlines	Dallas (DFW) 2023-10-18 20:20	Rome (FCO) 2023-10-19 18:45	15h 25m	1	Click to book

↺ Regenerate

If you'd like more or fewer options, just let me know!

At first, I wasn't impressed with the list of flights ChatGPT listed. First, it only generated one-way tickets, but by doubling the cost of the one-way price and then checking on Google flights, the cost of the flights wasn't too far off. In fact, it was pretty close to accurate when I accounted for baggage costs. This is great considering how fast it was for me to use ChatGPT to do the initial research.

Chapter Fifteen

Battling Glamping Phobias

Planning Your Travel Route

Traveling with friends is my favorite way to travel. I know many people don't feel the same way as I do. In fact, many feel the exact opposite, but for me, it's the best way to travel! When you have friends that vibe with the way you travel, it can be so much fun! I have been fortunate enough to have several friends like that. One couple is great at camping. Since I know nothing about camping, it's nice to go with them, because they more or less organize everything.

When we set off for our digital nomad life, one of the saddest things we had to give up was our frequent camping trips with our friends. Now, I am considering taking a month or two to Glamp or caravan around, something we have, until this point, not attempted in our full-time travel.

I am nervous about the prospect. Different travel requires different expertise. Although it can be quite doable to learn these different expertise, it's a little intimidating when starting off. In my case, if I mess up, I could be without internet for several days. As a full-time freelancer, that could be a real problem. So before I do that kind of travel, I'm going to be using ChatGPT.

Let's pretend I'm doing it next month and find a perfect route for a caravan trip across Norway.

The Priming

"You are a travel expert who specializes in camper and caravan travel throughout Europe. You know all of the routes, all of the campsites, and all of the hookup spots. When I ask you questions, you will answer them thoroughly. Because you're an expert traveler, you'll make recommendations I may not have specifically requested. Do you understand?"

The Prompt

"I want to start and end my caravan road trip in Oslo. I'm going to go on a 10-day caravan trip with my spouse. Please generate a recommended route with five to eight different locations. I want you to consider caravan hookups, campsites with showers and bathrooms, beautiful things to see, plenty to do, and anything you can think of a person traveling in a caravan for 10 days would want or need. Before getting started, do you have questions for me?"

The last question is especially important because I don't know a lot about caravanning, so I don't know even what preferences to input because I've never done it before. Something I would also want to ask is:

"How much do you think it would cost for a 10-day caravanning trip across Norway?"

"What are some activities in [input the areas ChatGPT recommended]?"

"What are some of the typical challenges caravaners may face, and what do you recommend doing to avoid them?"

Based on what I learned about what ChatGPT fed me, I will take 5 to 10 minutes of additional research to verify. ChatGPT is famous for making the occasional mistake, so it's always important to do a little fact-checking before moving forward with your actual plans. In this stage, I've only spent maybe five minutes doing research, so correcting an error or two in my notes is no big deal, versus finding out there was a mistake after making reservations, buying the caravan, buying flights to Norway, etc.

Chapter Sixteen

Go Weird or Go Home

Finding Unique Things to Do

L et's talk about how you can use AI to plan them.

First, start by choosing your destination. Once you have chosen your location, you feed ChatGPT your preferences, budget, and the types of activities you prefer (hiking trails, kayaking tours, or even adventure sports, sightseeing, museums, restaurants, and/or historical landmarks, etc).

Personally, I almost never plan activities before I go on vacation. Some of you are rereading the last sentence and doing a lot of incredulous blinking, I know, but I'm just not that big on planning. I love a certain amount of spontaneity.

When I get to a new place, I walk around and explore, but as the month moves on, I have to hunt for more unique or unusual activities. By then, I'd typically already visited all the famous attractions.

To find new activities, either I jump on Google Maps, filter for attractions, and look at what is close by, or I have to scour a bunch of blogs. The problem is, going through blogs is time consuming and the first 10 to 15 things are typically the activities I've already done. I either have to look for extra-long lists or go through a bunch of them and read the last few things on their list to get anything different.

Conveniently, ChatGPT can do it all for me. Let's try it out.

The Priming

"You are an expert traveler and travel agent. You are great at finding things to do in Da Nang, Vietnam for couples that are both unique and fun. You're great at finding things that are unusual and not typically listed on the top one to 10 things to do in Da Nang. You think like a local, because you're so experienced and well traveled in this city. Do you understand?"

The Prompt

"Generate a detailed list of the top 25 things to do in Da Nang, Vietnam. These things will be unique and interesting and perfect for couples to do. Please shortly describe what each activity is. Include the location, the distance from Son Tra, their hours of operation, and the cost."

Now, I have a list including some of the top lists, but now also includes a dozen or so things I've not even heard of. Many times ChatGPT will include a link to purchase, but I will often search on Klook or Google for discounted ticket prices.

Chapter Seventeen

From Napkin Scribbles ...to Official Itinerary

How to Use ChatGPT to Create Usable Itineraries

I have never used an itinerary in my life. However, I personally know many people who have and some who are even required to have it. My family, for example, is mostly military. Fun fact, soldiers need to submit an itinerary to the military before they can travel. They need to know if one of their soldiers is in an area where there's a disaster, or if they need to recall a soldier to active duty, where they can find them.

When I was planning my wedding, several family members needed to create an itinerary before traveling. When I looked at my brother's itinerary made by his research-savvy wife, my stomach tied into knots. It was *extremely* detailed. She had carefully logged every activity, even noting the travel time in between each.

In their case, the military needed an itinerary of their trip outside of the USA, but it also suited my brother's and his wife's personalities. Planning ahead saved my brother and his wife a lot of money and stress. It took my sister-in-law a long time to create her plans, but thankfully, you can have ChatGPT create a detailed itinerary for you within a few minutes.

The Priming

"You are an expert travel agent and especially well-versed in creating travel itineraries that are both detailed and accurate. You consider travel times and start times and prices for activities as well as things I may not have thought of as a customer. Do you understand?"

The Prompt

"Generate a detailed itinerary for my trip to Fiji. Before getting started, what questions do you have for me?"

This is a quick way of getting started. Ideally, ChatGPT asks you all the questions that would prompt the perfect itinerary. If you notice it's missing one or two things, you can either manually add it when you copy and paste ChatGPT's response into your Word document, or you can have ChatGPT rewrite the itinerary after it's complete and prompt it with the missing information.

Tripit

For keeping track of the plans I make, I like to use an app called Tripit.com. As I plan and book things, I update this app, which is linked to my Google calendar. The easiest way to update the app is by forwarding confirmation emails to it.

There is a free plan and a pro plan. I have invested the $49 annual fee for the pro plan because I travel so much, but many people can get by with the free plan. Once I have a flight, hotel, or transportation confirmation, I will forward the email directly to the app.

I can even save the ticket (or any travel documents I need, such as an e-visa, for example) into the plan details inside the app. You can access information offline, making it super handy for going through customs in a country you don't have cell service. However, if you don't want the app, you can copy the

ChatGPT's response into a Word document and either print it and/or save it on your phone to reference later.

Chapter Eighteen
I Forgot I Had a Dog

How to Seamlessly Prep to Leave

"I forgot I had a dog."

I had to read the text a few times before it sunk in. It was the day before our trip and my friend was scrambling to find someone to watch her sweet, elderly Pitbull named Jack.

Prepping to leave is a weirdly skipped-over topic for most travel bloggers and experts. For most, it's not considered part of the trip, and in a sense, that's kinda true, but the chaos that often ensues before a trip — marring the trip's memory — can often be avoided.

Many people dislike checklists, but they have been scientifically proven to help people remember more. In fact, a surgeon by the name of Atul Gawande wrote a book called "The Checklist Manifesto: How to Get Things Right". He adopted the use of checklists for his operations to avoid making mistakes. He admitted he was human and things could get missed.

Even experts, entirely focused on what they do best, can make mistakes and miss things. Miscommunications happen. And tiny mistakes can have huge implications. So if you are misfortunate enough to have one right before a trip, you could start your journey feeling flustered, furious, or heartbroken that you have to stop the trip altogether.

So, mom or dad with a million things on your plate, cut yourself some slack and make a checklist so you don't miss something important.

Let me tell you, being a "travel expert" does not exempt you from making mega mistakes. It was Saturday afternoon, and I remembered I hadn't printed my Vietnam e-Visa. "It's an e-Visa," you say. "Why would you need to print it?" Good question! Vietnam, I'll leave you to unravel that mystery, but all I know is that even though they don't need to write anything on it, stamp it, or keep it, the guards at the border are incapable of reading the information off of my phone and must have the same document printed out.

As I remembered this inconvenient fact, my stomach dropped. It was Saturday, and we needed to print something. I was in the middle of packing my entire apartment to leave the next day, and I had to scramble across town to find a printer. Fun fact, Vietnam and Google Maps are not talking. I went to three different places — all closed despite the lies told on my map app.

Worse, the traffic was ATROCIOUS. Turns out, the city was putting on a fireworks show - the last of the season — and all of Da Nang wanted to see it. I am not exaggerating when I say it took 3 1/2 hours to fail at a task that should have only taken 30 minutes, max. Needless to say, we were not in a good mood when we returned to the apartment sweaty and empty-handed.

We ended up finding a printing place near the border (not listed on Google Maps, but pointed out by our helpful hotel attendant), but it added a chaotic element to our border run. What's worse was it was entirely avoidable. I was busy and missed a small, teenie-weeny detail that threw our entire experience into full-blown, panicky chaos.

You don't want to remember, last minute like a friend of mine did, that "Oh, yeah... we have a dog. We need someone to watch him." It sounds obvious, but there are a million things that need to be done before a vacation. Forgetting a detail is never out of the question, no matter how savvy a traveler you are. My friend travels all the time and always has someone set to watch her pup. She was an experienced traveler. This was probably her half-a-dozenth trip that year.

It happens.

A checklist can help. Have ChatGPT help you make one.

The Priming

"You are an expert traveler and you always remember to do everything you need to do before you leave. You are great at creating to-do lists for those prepping to go on vacation so they can have a smooth travel experience both leaving and coming home. Do you understand?"

The Prompt

"ChatGPT, help me create a comprehensive to-do list of things I need to do before leaving for vacation. Consider my specific needs including work-related tasks, home preparation, tasks for my children not joining the vacation, tasks for my children joining the vacation, electronic preparations (including downloading an e-SIM app, printing out tickets, getting a local taxi app, and more), medical preparations (including getting prescriptions filled and filling a vitamin slash medication pill box), vehicle preparations, pet preparations, document preparations, etc. Before moving forward, what questions do you have for me?"

Fill out any questions ChatGPT has for you and you'll have a vacation prep checklist that will ensure leaving for your vacation is as smooth and seamless as possible!

Chapter Nineteen

4 Books & No Toothbrush

How to Make Perfect Packing Lists

The conundrum of packing during such an overwhelming time as right before a vacation can lead someone to pack four books they will not read ...but forget their toothbrush.

Checklists, baby. They can be magic in helping people remember to pack everything. Even an experienced traveler can forget important stuff!

Ever search for something eight times in the same place, knowing for certain that THIS time, the thing you are missing will turn up?

...or is that just me?

I stared into my suitcase and looked through it one MORE time, just to be sure. Nope... I hadn't brought a toothbrush, soap, shampoo, or any socks.

What *did* I bring? I mean, seriously.

I forgot almost everything I needed for this little mini trip I had booked. True, Hoi An was only an hour and a half drive from Da Nang. I could technically go back or buy the forgotten items in a nearby grocery store, but even so... it was ridiculous. I'm an expert traveler. I travel full time, for heaven's sake. How did I forget toothpaste???

It's because I didn't create a packing list. I could have done this in a few seconds on ChatGPT, but my ego took the reins and left the toothbrush behind.

How to use ChatGPT to create a packing list.

The Priming

"ChatGPT, you are an expert traveler and travel agent. You are specialized in creating thorough packing lists that anticipate the needs of the traveler in each specific location. Do you understand?"

The Prompt

"Generate a packing list for a one-night, two-day trip to Hoi An during the month of July. This packing list will be for a couple who will not be doing any extra activities outside of walking around town in hot temperatures. Before answering, what questions do you have for me?"

Getting a quick little packing list would've been all I needed to remember everything for my trip... I highly recommend you do the same.

Chapter Twenty

Dealing With ChatDiva

Tips on Improving Your ChatGPT Responses

C hatGPT can be a bit of a diva at times, but knowing how to finesse it can make a world of difference.

Expect a Mistake or Two

ChatGPT is famous for its mistakes. If it doesn't know or understand something, it will make it up. Soon, that will change I am sure, but for now, we are stuck with an imperfect travel assistant. However, with the right prompting and nudging, you can get 90-95% accuracy.

I recommend taking your time to prime the chat. Have it ask you questions to best understand your preference, and do quick fact-checks when it spits out search results. I truly believe that even with the occasional mistakes, most of the travel planning is quicker with ChatGPT than doing individual searches through blog posts and articles.

Advanced Models & Plugins

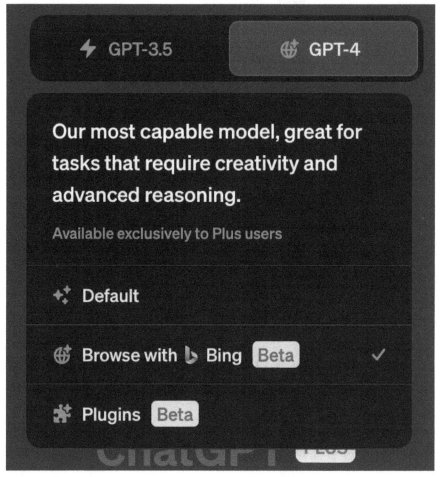

Right now, ChatGPT 4 is the advanced model. If you can swing the $20/month (at least for the months you're planning your trip), you can have access to advanced features such as plugins.

I recommend taking advantage as they have some travel-specific plugins that can make a difference in your search results. To take advantage of plugins, upgrade your account. Open a new thread, select ChatGPT 4, and at the top, select plugins and scroll down to the plugin store. I recommend searching the words: "flights", "accommodations", "browsing/search crawlers", and "travel".

Add as many plugins as you think will be helpful. A plugin that supports "prompting" might also be helpful when getting started to make the prompting process a little more intuitive.

Once you have added your plugins, you will have to select three plugins for your thread. Depending on what I am searching for, will determine which I select. To select a new plugin after you have started asking ChatGPT questions, you will have to open a new thread, so keep this in mind.

If you're lost, do a quick search on Google or YouTube, and you should be able to find updated, step-by-step instructions on finding good plugins, upgrading your account, and more. Again, they are updating ChatGPT every few weeks and they may have moved stuff around. A quick Google search should set you right.

Use a Desktop

I highly recommend using the desktop version instead of the mobile version, as that's limited.

Stop the Chat

Sometimes, ChatGPT will start auto-generating a response instead of asking you questions or letting you input your preferences. You can either let it finish and see if it guessed what you were trying to say or, I like to hit "stop generating" and clarify what I am inputting.

Edit Previous Responses

If ChatGPT goes rogue or you submit a response inadvertently (easy to do), you can go back and edit your response. Either wait until ChatGPT finishes responding or hit "stop generating" if needed. Go to the message you need to change, hit edit (right now, it looks like a pen and paper icon next to your response), type in your new response, and resubmit it.

Questions

Asking ChatGPT questions and having it do the same for you is one of the secret weapons to getting the best results with your AI research.

<u>Chat-to-You Examples</u>

Thank you for providing those details. They will help in crafting a personalized priming prompt for your travel planning needs. Before we move forward, I would like to know a few more things:

1. Do you have a preference for a certain part of the world or are you open to any location globally?
2. What is your preferred mode of transportation during your vacation? (for example: public transit, rental car, bike, etc.)
3. Do you have any specific health or accessibility considerations I should be aware of while planning?
4. Do you have any preferences when it comes to the climate or time of year to travel?
5. Is there anything else you think might be important to consider while planning this vacation?

Your answers to these additional questions will help in refining the AI's responses to better suit your preferences.

"In a minute, I am going to ask you [to find accommodations, plan a camper road trip route, etc.]. Before I do so, what questions do you have for me in order for you to generate the best results?"

You-to-Chat Examples

 you are starting to give me strange answers back. What do you need from me to get you back on track?

"[Insert question or prime] (followed immediately by): Do you understand?"

"You seemed to have forgotten I am [searching for a beach location, for example] Do you remember my preferences? Please repeat them so I know you remember them all."

Start a New Chat

Every once in a while, ChatGPT forgets everything and says some wild stuff.

You can try prompting it back on track, but I find it's easier to start a new chat thread.

Staying Organized

Let's talk for a minute about keeping organized. Traveling has a lot of moving parts to it. You don't want to take the time to plan your entire trip and then lose your flight confirmation.

Day One App (Free or $34.00/year)

I am OBSESSED with the Day One app. It's a journal app I use all the time. One of my favorite features is the Notebook feature. I create different notebooks to capture different things. One sends my Instagram feed to it. You won't realize how valuable that is until you get your profile shut down for no reason. — Just ask the thousands of people who had their accounts suspended because of a technical glitch.

But, the real reason I use it is for the other notebooks. I have one for travel notes (for finding good deals, finding great new spots to visit, etc.), one I use as a travel journal (for uploading travel stories and images), one is for keeping track of my novel notes (short story ideas, character development, etc.), and one is for learning new things (taking notes on webinars I watch, linking resources and tools, and even uploading full PDFs and eBooks).

I love that it gives me offline access to my journals, so if you choose to upload your travel docs, you can still access them even if Wi-Fi is an issue. You can search your notebooks, another thing that is unbelievably handy, especially when you're in a hurry and trying to find a small detail.

Tripit App (Free or $49/year)

As I mentioned in an earlier chapter, Tripit app (or Tripit.com) is an absolute MUST for me. It is an amazing tool for organization. I use Day One for planning, but once my plans are set, I upload the plans into the Tripit app.

Once you get the confirmation for a flight, you can forward the confirmation to plans@tripit.com and it will automatically create a flight tracker into the app. Once a flight plan is created in the app, you can upload tickets when you get them, e-Visa info, if needed, and any documents you will use at the airport to get through security and on your flight. During COVID travel, this was quite a lot of documents and it was so handy to have everything for all travelers in my app in an easy-to-locate spot.

Once a flight plan is in the app, Tripit will update you with changes to the flights, remind you to check into your flight, track miles you earn (premium plan), and even remind you when to leave for the airport. Once at the airport, you can use an interactive map of the airport on the app. During your flight, it can track your progress. I've run into the occasional glitch, but overall, it's been the best tool for keeping organized.

I'll link both apps, and more, on RobotsDoStuff.com.

ONE LAST THING...

Thank you sooooo much for reading! If you enjoyed this book, I'd be very grateful if you'd post a short review on Amazon and on Goodreads. Your support really does make a difference!

Search for this book title by Angelina Allsop to leave your review.

Thanks again for your support!

About the Author

"To have a life full of robots and monsters is to have a full life, indeed."
-Angelina Allsop

My name is Angelina Allsop and I am the proud author of such thrilling tales as "*How to Tell if Your Grandma is a Vampire*", "*The Death & Life of Peter Green*" series, as well as my clumsy exploration of Ai in the "*Robots Did it*" series.

When I am not arguing with robots, negotiating with monsters, or swatting away bats, I am petting a stray dog, poking crabs at the beach, and exploring the world with my hubby.

Together, we happily wander from country to country, getting fat on the local grub and learning about the ghosts and ghouls that live in the area.

Keep in Touch

Get FREE books for kids at FreeBooks4Kids.com and FREE AI resources (and more) at RobotsDoStuff.com. Find my books and a ton of free stuff at AngelinaAllsop.com.

Eeee!! Thanks for reading. I can't tell you what it means to me!

www.ingramcontent.com/pod-product-compliance
Lightning Source LLC
Chambersburg PA
CBHW071551080326
40690CB00056B/1791